YOUNG PROFILES

Enrique Iglesias

Jill C. Wheeler
ABDO Publishing Company

visit us at
www.abdopub.com

Published by ABDO Publishing Company, 4940 Viking Drive, Edina, Minnesota 55435.
Copyright © 2003 by Abdo Consulting Group, Inc. International copyrights reserved in all
countries. No part of this book may be reproduced in any form without written permission
from the publisher.

Printed in the United States.

Cover Photo: Corbis
Interior Photos: Corbis pp. 7, 9, 11, 13, 15, 17, 19, 25, 27, 28-29, 31;
    Image Direct pp. 5, 21, 23

Editors: Kate A. Conley, Kristin Van Cleaf, Kristianne E. Vieregger
Art Direction: Neil Klinepier

Library of Congress Cataloging-in-Publication Data

Wheeler, Jill C., 1964-
    Enrique Iglesias / Jill C. Wheeler.
       p. cm. -- (Young profiles)
    Includes bibliographical references (p.) and index.
    Summary: Discusses the life and career of the Hispanic American singing star.
    ISBN 1-57765-993-7
     1. Iglesias, Enrique, 1975---Juvenile literature. 2. Singers--United
States--Biography--Juvenile literature. [1. Iglesias, Enrique, 1975- 2. Singers. 3. Spanish
Americans--Biography.] I. Title. II. Series.

ML3930.I39 W47 2003
782.42164'092--dc21
[B]
                                                                    2002027798

Contents

Enrique!

Enrique Iglesias first entered the music scene in 1995. Since then, he's taken the **Latin** music world by storm. In a three-year period, he sold more Spanish-language albums than any other Latin singer during that time.

Like many other Latin artists, Enrique sings from the heart. He combines his **lyrics** with simple, upbeat pop-music melodies. The result is a new twist on the traditional Latin style. It has captured a whole new **audience** of young people.

Today, Enrique Iglesias is an international superstar. He has recorded in English, Spanish, Italian, and Portuguese. Fans from around the world scream, and even cry, at the sight of the handsome, dark-eyed singer.

Fans scream for Enrique at a concert celebrating the beginning of the National Football League's season.

Profile of a Singing Star

Name: Enrique Iglesias
Date of Birth: May 8, 1975
Place of Birth: Madrid, Spain
Height: Six feet, two inches
Pet: Grammy, a golden retriever
Parents: Julio Iglesias and Isabel Preysler
Siblings: Isabel (Chabeli) and Julio Jr.
Job: Singer and songwriter
Current Home: Miami, Florida
Hobbies: Windsurfing, waterskiing, jet skiing, and scuba diving
Marital Status: Single
Favorite Foods: Chicken McNuggets, French fries, and pizza
Favorite Musicians: Dire Straits, Fleetwood Mac, Journey, Bruce Springsteen, and Billy Joel

Albums: *Enrique Iglesias* (1995), *Vivir* (1997), *Cosas Del Amor* (1998), *Enrique* (1999), *Escape* (2001), *Quizás* (2002)

Quote from Enrique: "Try to live happy every day."

Musical Roots

Enrique Iglesias was born on May 8, 1975, in Madrid, Spain. His father is **Latin** singing star Julio Iglesias. His mother, Isabel Preysler, is a former model from the Philippines.

Enrique has two older **siblings**. He has a sister, Isabel, who is nicknamed Chabeli. He also has a brother named Julio Jr.

As children, Enrique and his siblings didn't see their father often. The famous singer was usually on the road performing concerts. All of this time apart was difficult for the family. Enrique's parents divorced when he was only three years old.

After the divorce, Enrique, Chabeli, and Julio Jr. stayed at their home in Spain. Their father moved to Miami, Florida. Soon, the Iglesias children began spending their summers in Miami.

Back in Spain, Enrique's mother had remarried and begun a career as a journalist. By then, Enrique was in school and had adjusted to his new life. But that life changed on December 20, 1981. That day, **Basque separatists** kidnapped Enrique's grandfather and held him for **ransom**.

Enrique's grandfather was eventually rescued. However, Enrique's parents feared that their children might be kidnapped, too. So they decided the children should join their father in Miami.

Enrique with his mother and father

A New Life

Miami became Enrique's new home, but he missed his mother. "Leaving my mother, it was very hard," he told a journalist. "And having to start a new life, new friends, new school, different language. It wasn't easy." He visited Madrid often, and his mother came to Miami several times a year.

In Miami, Enrique lived a privileged life. There was always plenty of money. Enrique's family lived in a nice house. However, his father didn't spend much time there. "I just saw him work hard," Enrique said of his father.

Enrique talked with both of his parents regularly. Yet he wasn't as close to them as he would have liked. His nanny, Elvira Olivares, became a mother figure to him. He was closer to her than to anyone else.

Enrique usually didn't share his thoughts with anyone. Instead, he wrote them in his journal. When he was 13, he

Enrique and his mother, Isabel Preysler

began writing his thoughts in the form of song **lyrics**. "It was the only way I had to express myself," he said. "I had nobody to talk to. I'd pick up a piece of paper and write some lyrics."

Secret Dreams

In Miami and in Madrid, Enrique was an average teenager. No one guessed he had wanted to be a singer since childhood. "When I was seven, I would kneel in bed and pray I'd be a singer," Enrique remembers.

Enrique didn't say anything to his family about his dream, however. "I didn't want anything negative. It was my thing," he said. "Even now, I have my career very separated from my family."

Though Enrique kept it to himself, he continued working toward his dream. He listened to popular artists, such as Journey and Dire Straits. They inspired him as he continued to write his own songs.

Eventually, Enrique started high school at the Gulliver Preparatory School. He describes himself as having been very

Enrique sings with all of his heart.

shy and usually on his own. Besides writing songs, he continued to enjoy two of his favorite sports, windsurfing and waterskiing.

When Enrique was 15, he began practicing with two local musicians. They helped him improve his singing and songwriting skills.

At first, the musicians didn't know Enrique's father was a famous singer. Enrique kept this a secret. He wanted to be successful because of his own talent, rather than his father's fame. So even after the musicians discovered who Enrique's father was, they kept it a secret.

Enrique graduated from high school in 1993. He still wanted to be a performer. But his father wanted him to attend college. So Enrique enrolled at the University of Miami to study business.

Enrique spent about a year taking classes at the university. However, his heart was never in it. He decided to drop out of the university to focus on his music.

Enrique likes to write in his room late at night. If he still likes the song the next day, he knows he has something special.

Enrique Martinez

Enrique already knew a lot about the music business from watching his father. He knew he needed a smart manager. So he asked for a secret meeting with his father's former manager, Fernan Martinez.

Fernan was surprised when Enrique shared his dream of becoming a singer. But when Enrique sang for him, Fernan noticed the same talent that had made Enrique's father a star.

There was just one problem. Enrique refused to use his real name on his **demo** tape. Fernan was surprised. Enrique's family name would provide many special opportunities. But Enrique wanted to succeed based on his own talents.

Because of this, Enrique made his Spanish-language demo under the name Enrique Martinez. Fernan told record company executives that this new singer was from Colombia.

At first, several record companies turned down Enrique. Finally, he submitted his **demo** to the executives at Fonovisa. It is a small, Spanish-language record company. They signed Enrique to a three-album deal for $1 million. All three albums would be in Spanish.

Enrique worked hard to become a famous singer.

Enrique Iglesias

Enrique went to Toronto, Canada, to record. Five months later, he finished his **debut** album. He had written many of the songs when he was a teenager. In fact, he **dedicated** the album to his former nanny, Elvira Olivares.

With his recording contract established, Enrique decided it was finally the right time to tell the world who he was. So he titled his first album *Enrique Iglesias*. But now he had to find the right time to tell his parents about his career choice.

Enrique's parents were surprised to learn their son had not been studying business at the university. His father was upset that Enrique had not consulted him. Enrique had to explain that he needed to succeed on his own. Even though Enrique had kept his dream a secret, his parents were proud of him.

Enrique Iglesias was shipped to stores in September 1995. It was an immediate hit, selling more than 1 million copies in three months. Enrique received a Grammy Award for Best **Latin** Pop Performance for this album. *Billboard* magazine also named him Artist of the Year. The 21-year-old star had become the best-selling Latin singer of 1996.

Enrique poses for cameras after winning his first Grammy Award.

World Tour

Enrique soon began work on his second album. He released *Vivir* in 1997. The Spanish word *vivir* means "to live." *Vivir* sold more than 1 million copies in just four months.

Enrique soon began his first world tour. It was a new challenge for the budding star. Performing live is very different from recording in a studio. Enrique had to learn how to be an entertainer, as well as a singer.

The tour was a huge success. Enrique performed nearly 80 concerts in more than 13 countries around the world, including the United States. More than 700,000 fans came to see the handsome young star in person.

The show itself was spectacular. The light and sound equipment alone filled two cargo jets. Some of Enrique's talented band members had worked with stars such as Elton John, Bruce Springsteen, and Billy Joel. The fans loved the show. Even the critics agreed Enrique Iglesias had something special.

  Billboard magazine named *Vivir* Album of the Year. The American Society of Composers, Authors, and Publishers gave Enrique a Best Composer Award. In addition, he began receiving invitations to appear on television shows.

Enrique appears on The Tonight Show with Jay Leno.

New Frontiers

After the tour, Enrique soon recorded his third album. This album of **ballads** showed Enrique's sensitive side. The album was called *Cosas Del Amor*, which means "matters of love" in Spanish. The album was released in September 1998.

Cosas Del Amor fulfilled Enrique's contract with Fonovisa. Now, many of the recording labels that had turned him down earlier were eager to sign him. Enrique wanted to break into the English-speaking market. He soon got his chance.

In 1999, actor and singer Will Smith saw Enrique in concert and was impressed. He asked Enrique to sing a song for the sound track for his new movie, *Wild Wild West*.

Enrique agreed, and he recorded "Bailamos," which means "we dance" in Spanish. "Bailamos" was also released as a **single**, which immediately shot up *Billboard*'s Hot 100 chart. Eventually, it made it to number one.

The **single**'s success gave Enrique the chance he needed. Interscope Records signed him to a six-album deal. *Enrique*, a completely English album, was Enrique's first album with Interscope Records. The album has gone **gold** or **platinum** in 32 countries.

Enrique's music has captured the hearts of fans all over the world.

New Opportunities

Enrique's success continued after "Bailamos" and *Enrique*. In January 2000, he sang with Christina Aguilera at the Super Bowl XXXIV halftime show. That same year, he began a world tour for his album *Enrique*.

Enrique released the album *Escape* in 2001. It had more of a rock-and-roll sound than his other albums. He had wanted to do an album with different musical styles. He knew that if he liked the music, his **audience** would, too.

Enrique also performed the song "Hero" at the *America: A Tribute to Heroes* event in 2001. Originally, he wrote the song with a different meaning. But he believes that it's good if one of his songs can be something positive for people.

Enrique sings with Christina Aguilera at the Super Bowl in 2000.

Stay Tuned

Despite the fame and long hours, Enrique tries to lead a normal life. "I walk around all . . . day in a T-shirt, jeans, and [with] eight dollars in my pocket," he says. He also still loves water sports. Once, he accidentally hit a tree while water-skiing and needed 40 stitches!

When he's not relaxing, Enrique is busy working. He is acting in a movie called *Once Upon a Time in Mexico*. It is due to be released in 2003. Enrique is also busy with his music. He released an all-Spanish album, *Quizás*, in 2002. *Quizás* means "perhaps" in Spanish.

Through it all, Enrique has remained true to himself and his music. "What I want when I listen to music is what everyone wants. That it take me someplace else, make me happy or sad or remember a feeling," he says. "Music changes you."

Enrique on the set of his new movie

Glossary

audience - a group of people watching a performance.

ballad - a slow, romantic, or sentimental song.

Basque separatists - members of a group that want a separate government for the Basque people. They often use violence and kidnappings to obtain money and awareness for their cause.

debut - a first appearance.

dedicate - to give a message showing affection or thanks in an album, book, or other artistic work.

demo - a recording made to demonstrate the talent of a singer.

gold - when more than 500,000 copies of an album are sold.

Latin - of or relating to the people, culture, or language of Central and South America, which are also known as Latin America.

lyrics - the words of a song.

platinum - when more than 1 million copies of an album are sold.

ransom - money demanded in return for the release of someone or something in captivity.

sibling - a brother or sister.

single - one song from an album, sold by itself.

Web Sites

Would you like to learn more about Enrique Iglesias? Please visit **www.abdopub.com** for up-to-date Web site links about Enrique's life and his music. These sites are routinely monitored and updated to provide the most current information available.

Index